Fly High My Kite

Margaret Penner Toews

Published by
Milton and Margaret Toews
Box 369
Neilburg, Saskatchewan
Canada S0M 2C0

Printed in U.S.A. by
Lee Printing, Burns, Kansas 66840
1982

Cover design by Irvin Amundrud
Illustrations by Ralph Friesen

Special thanks to Lydda Regehr for her
assistance with the harmony in "Accept Our
Thanks, O Lord" and "Samson"

Contents

Dedication

To the little troop of grandchildren following us: Ranae, Jamie, Andrew, Cory, Trevor, and any others who might join their ranks, with a prayer that their kite strings will never get too tangled nor their sails too torn to fly.

Fly High, My Kite

Fly high, my kite,
  fly free, fly high,
One with the cloud
  in the blue, blue sky,
One with the eagles that soar and dive,
Dipping and whipping like a thing alive.

    Fly high, my kite,
      fly full, fly high
    Where the air is clean
      in a sun-lit sky.
    You are anchored tight in my sturdy hand.
    White sail, fly high, by the spring-wind
      fanned.

Fly high, my heart,
  fly free, fly full
On the winds of God
  with their upward pull.
Fly high over evil, high over wrong,
As I reel out a line of a glad new song.

    Up, up it soars to reach the light!
    I think about prayer as I fly my kite!

I Wonder . . .

I'm here,
   and I wonder where I've been.
Where did the I
   that is me begin?

Poems for the Wee Folk

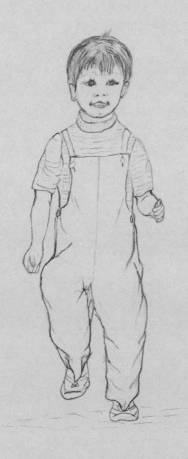

Here I come, world!
I'm brand new!
What have you got
for me to do?

I Wonder

I sit on Grandpa's lap
And snuggle on his breast
And run my fingers through his beard
And gently rest.

I sit on Grandpa's lap
And wonder if it's odd
That when I snuggle close to him
I think of God?

My Grandpa Loves Me

All Dressed

Sweater
Dress
Shoes
Socks
Clips and holders
For my locks
Coat
Mittens
Furry boot
Snugly scarf
Wooly toque

Oh, yes!
Now my smile.

All dressed!

Hi There!

Bow-wow! Share with Me!

12

Creating

Every baby clean and sweet,
Tiny fingers, tickly feet;
Every kitten, soft as silk,
Learning how to lap its milk;
Every chick whose yellow beak
Pecks a hole through which to peek;
Every pup as smooth as satin;
Every pea that starts to fatten;
Every bud that bursts in bloom;
Every sticky, brown cocoon
Opening up and sprouting wings;
Every meadowlark that sings,
Tell us God keeps on—and on—
Creating things.

Animal Fare!

I look at the monkey,
I look at the bear,
And I look at the cat
  with a long, hard stare.
I poke at the eyes
  of the horse and the sheep.
The fat little pig
  looks half asleep.

Then I eat up the monkey.
I eat up the bear.
I eat up the cat
  and the camels (a pair).
I gobble the horse
  and the sheep and the ox—

Oh! Oh! I just emptied
The animal-cracker box!

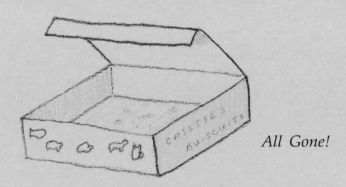

All Gone!

They Always Keep Telling Me

Don't touch the flowers.
Don't you jump.
Don't smear the walls.
Don't make a thump.
Don't pull the curtain.
Don't act smart.
Don't ask the lady
For another tart.
Don't make faces.
Don't chase flies.
Put away that stickpin,
And don't poke their eyes.
Don't scatter crayons.
Don't be rude.
Darling, don't just
Sit and brood.
Don't you cry, dear.
Don't you pout.
Stop saying, "Mom, now
Let's get OUT."
What IS a little
Child to do?
I don't know.
Do you?

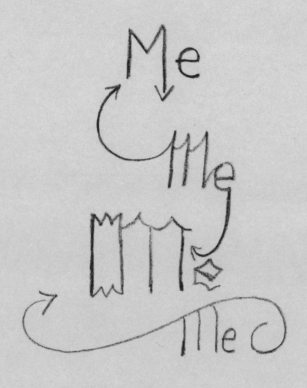

If you want to be liked by no one,
Here's all you that do, you see,
Talk about, think about, care about
Nothing but *I* and *Me*.

Downtown with Mommy

Don't hurry so, Mommy!
You're yanking my hand.
My legs are so tired;
Oh, please understand!
Each step that you take
Means I have to make three.
Please, Mommy, slow down!
I want to catch up with ME!

Three Years Old

I try to sit in Sunday School.
I try hard not to giggle.
I try to leave my itch alone.
I try to quit to wiggle.

The teacher says God knows all things.
He sees me with His eye.
Oh, goody! Then He also knows
How very hard I *try*.

Puddle Poem!

Puddles are made to look at the sky in
and watch the clouds wiggle the minute you pry in
it with a small stick.
Then you watch the stick float.
Next you stir with it, watching the puddle
get thick.
Puddles like that must be splished in
and splashed in
(is anyone looking?), then meant to be
dashed in
with your bare feet.
Then you squeeze and you squish
the mud with your toes.
Next you make pies in it
(by that time the skies in it
have all disappeared).
First you stir with your stick,
then beat it and pat it,
and it's wondrously thick!
What fun!

And, then again, maybe it's better
when you see a puddle,
you put on your boots
and keep your feet dry
and just watch the clouds
and forget about pie
(and I think you know why.)

Puddles Were Made to Stir

Point of View

A tree is big.
        My daddy's small
beside a tree,
        and I am tall
beside my cutest
        cuddly doll.
My doll is big
        beside the bug
That scuttled 'cross
        the back door rug.
The bug is big
        beside the flea
That perched upon
        the peony—
A teeny-tiny one with wings.

I wonder how God looks at things.

Samantha

I'd like to tell you about my calf.
It's a she.
I call her Samantha 'cause that's her name.
There is no other calf that is quite the same.
She stands all quiet in the sun,
Then all of a sudden away she'll run
With tail flung high like a silly flag—
Galloping, leaping, and playing tag
(Or trying to!) with a lazy pig.
She'll stop right short and dance a jig.
If you could see
My little calf,
You'd laugh.

Calm Down, Samantha!

Can You
Tell Me Why?

Dandelion Questions

Can you tell me why
When daffodils smile
It is something so special?
Why are *they* so worthwhile?
I, a poor dandelion,
Just as gay, just as yellow,
Am frowned on and thought of
As a bad little fellow.
I bloom just as gaily—
Give such generous seeds!
Why are daffodils "flowers"
And dandelions "just weeds"?

Poof!

27

Suffer the Children . . .

The little ones took turns upon His lap
And leaned against the Lord all unafraid,
And, as He sat and rested on a stone,
A trusting head against His heart was laid.

He must have dearly loved the little children
Just as He loves them now and always sees us;
So, while I pray, I close my eyes, a-thinking
It's *me* that's resting in the arms of Jesus.

Little Lisa Tells Her Mom All about What Happened in School Today

Today the girls were naughty.
They yanked the braids of Dotty,
And I knew they'd like it if I did it, too,
But I thought of what you'd said—
What if I were in her stead,
Just what would I want Dotty then to do?
So I put my hand in hers
(Quarrels always are a curse!),
And I said, "Let's all of us go out and play."
So they left the braids of Dotty,
And no longer were they naughty,
And we altogether had a super day!

Some Children Don't

Do you have lots of toys and things,
Balls and bats and dolls and swings,
Games and bikes and planes with wings?
    Some children don't.

Have you a home that is warm and neat
Where you always have lots of food to eat,
Where you play and pray and work and sleep?
    Some children don't.

Have you a mother who hugs you tight
And tucks you in with a kiss at night
And teaches you what is wrong and right?
    Some children don't.

Have you a dad who is good and kind
And cares enough to make you mind,
And you think he's the best you could ever find?
    Some children don't.

Do you go to a church where people care,
Where God is near and answers prayer,
And it really matters if you are there?
    Some children don't.

Do you know God knows each one by name
And He loves all children just the same?
Do you ever thank Him that Jesus came?
    Some children don't.

Twins

Mine and I-Want-It were two little boys,
And, oh, how they quarreled and fought!
They tugged at their toys till they tore them in two—
No matter what Mother had bought.

Mine called I-Want-It all kinds of bad names;
He said he was selfish and mean.
I-Want-It said Mine was an awful lot worse!
But *I* thought, It is plain to be seen

When they batter each other with fist and with
    tongue,
Neither of them ever wins,
And Mine is exactly as bad as I-Want-It;
For they are identical twins!

Grade Two

My teacher is the best! I *like* my teacher!
When I have tried real hard, she says, "That's
  great!"
She doesn't scold me even if I've smudged
And didn't get the lines exactly straight.

She says it matters mostly if I try.
She helps me with my boots and doesn't say
(When I have pulled like forty horses!), "My child!
You *are* a baby! There! Now go and play."

She likes me though I am a bit "behind."
I like her, too, because my teacher's kind.
      (I'm thinking, Jesus also was a teacher—
      He must have been much kinder yet than
        mine.)

Great-Grandpas
and Great-Grandmas

Great-grandmas are wonderful!
How do I know?
I learned all about them
A long time ago.

They've usually got candies
In pockets or purses.
They sit and they listen
To all of your verses.

They let you pick flowers
That bloom in their garden
And when you've been naughty,
They're eager to pardon.

They're handy to answer
A little girl's questions
And sometimes come up
With the nicest suggestions.

The one I like best
Is, "Come stay for awhile!"
Enough to make anyone
Burst with a smile.

But there's also another
Good thing I've found out!
Though great-grandmas are "great,"
And there isn't a doubt—

With their toys and their swings
And the things they make—
It is really the great-grandpas
Who take the cake!

Fish and Find . . .

Parable Poems

Fishermen

You've never been a fisherman?
Nor ever seen the sea?
But Jesus Christ is calling,
"Come! Come and fish with Me!"

Use the rod of courage.
Use the line of prayer,
Use the bait of friendship,
And reel them in with care.

Don't let the line get tangled
With selfishness and sin.
Come, all you eager children,
Let's go and fish with Him!

Banking

The youngster strode to the wicket.
The teller cocked his head.
"Young man, what is it you want?" he asked.
"Some money, of course," he said.

"Some money?" the teller queried
And, giving the boy a grin,
Said, "Son, I'm beginning to wonder,
Did you ever put any in?"

"Well, no-o-o," the youngster answered,
"But everyone surely knows
That the bank has a LOT of money—
Enough for all, I suppose."

"Sorry!" the teller answered.
"Before you can ever begin
To take money out of a bank,
You have to put money in."

Whatever you put into life,
There is one unchangeable law;
Later along in time,
That is just what you'll withdraw.

Deposit love and kindness,
Cheer and a sunny smile,
And those are the very coins
You'll get out of it after awhile.

There is also the Bank of Trouble.
It deals in spite and hate.
There you'll withdraw, with interest,
Great grief at a later date.

What is the name of your bank?
Is it Trouble on Joyless Lane?
Or is it the Bank of Cheer
On the corner of Mirth and Main?

BANK

*"I'd Like to
Have Money."*

Blue Day

I felt like kicking the footstool,
I felt like sassing my mom,
I felt like pinching the baby,
And nothing I did was fun.
I was sure that nobody loved me;
I sat and sulked on the stair,
And, bit by bit with my jacknife,
I whittled away on my hair.
I barked at my own pet dog,
And I kicked the family cat.

Blue Day!

The sight of my sister irked me;
My brother and I had a spat.
I got so tired of *me*,
And I thought I would like to die,
And then, perched there on the stairway,
I suddenly 'gan to cry.
Mom came and sat beside me;
She didn't say very much,
But I knew she must care a *little*
Just by her gentle touch.
"Let's pray together," she whispered.
"Dear Father, here is my boy;
He's unhappy and needs you badly.
Please touch him and give him joy."
Then placing a kiss on my forehead,
She asked me to help make buns
And said I was one of the nicest
Of her two freckled sons.
The thunder was suddenly over.
My day was no longer blue!
Can you tell me exactly what happens
When somebody prays for you?

My Kitty and I

My kitty and I (his name is Gondado)
    eat breakfast together at eight.
I have bacon and pancakes and porridge and eggs,
    And I sneak him some off of my plate.

My kitty and I have dinner at twelve.
    I feed him a bit 'neath the table—
A scrap of potato, a snippet of bread,
    and a tidbit of meat (if I'm able!).

My kitty and I, well, when we have supper,
    that's different! Gondado likes mice
And fish heads and gizzards and livers and lizards
    and other things equally nice.
I eat at the table, and he eats outside
    'neath the porch or the back door stair.
So when it is supper we eat, let me tell you,
    Gondado and I don't share.

My
Kitty
Gondado

Laziness

Lazy water! Never climbing,
Going where it's easiest,
Always going where it's quickest,
Even if it's crookedest.

Do you never climb and grapple?
What you please is what you do?
That is just how streams get crooked.
(Sad to say, and children, too!)

Poof!

"I'm biggest," said Bragger.
"I'm best," said Miss Pride.
"I'm greatest," said Boaster,
All puffed up inside.

Just three tiny pinpricks,
Then three puffing BOOMS,
And flat as a map
Lay the broken balloons!

This parable shows
When you're puffed up with pride,
Just a pinprick will tell
There is nothing inside.

So if you are tempted,
I'll give you a tip—
Just think of balloons
And button your lip!

Bragger Fell on His Face

The Mistaken Flea

An elephant crossed o'er a rickety bridge.
A flea followed hard in its wake,
And when they were over, the flea proudly said,
"My! how we did make that bridge shake!"

If you ever suppose you have done something great,
Remember, and make no mistake,
There is simply no good we can do without Christ—
It's not we who "made the bridge shake."

Cheer Up!

The Unhappy Leaf

A leaf on a tree
Once yearned to be free
From its twig—discontent with its lot,
But when it let go,
It no longer could grow,
And all it could do was rot.

Reconciled

If God has forgiven me
And God has forgiven you
And we have forgiven each other
And our hearts are clean and new
And both of us love Christ Jesus
With all that is in us, why!
We could not have a quarrel,
Even if we would try!

Where is God?

Where Is God?

Where is God?
As far as eye
can scan the reach
of sea and sky.

Where is God?
Where the oceans roar
and crash and break
on the rocky shore.

Where is God?
In every atom,
in every flower
as smooth as satin.

Where is God?
In the forest's gloom
where birches chatter
and cedars loom.

Where is God?
Where someone weeps
while others near,
uncaring, sleep.

Where is God?
Where a baby smiled;
for He lives in the heart
of each little child.

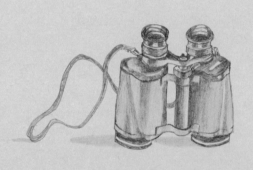

Learning

Questions in socials! Assignments in "lit!"
Even in spelling I'm boggled a bit.
Riddles in science that stretch the mind!
Pages of problems in math I find!

Then at home after school, my dad will say,
"Well, son, tell me, what did you learn today?"
I ponder and wonder and can't recall;
I don't really know what I learned at all.
I just did *problems* and answered queries
And worked at solutions till I was weary!
So how can I tell what came out of the churn?
Yet I realize little by little I learn.

In life I'll meet problems unpleasant and tough.
I'll try to remember, no matter how rough
The assignments I face, that each problem and test
Will help me to learn and to grow the best.

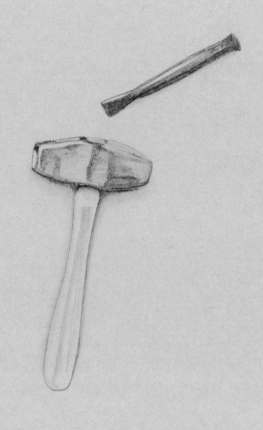

Two Jobs

There are always two jobs for a Christian to do;
For we're soldiers who work on a carpenter crew!
Muscled and brawny, sturdy and skilled,
We've a weapon to fight and a hammer to build.
We fight against giants that want to barge in—
Jealousy, hatred and anger and sin.

But that's not enough! We must also *do good*,
Building God's house—at least all of us *should*—
Helping the weak, being kind to the cross,
Loving the lonely, and seeking the lost.

Our swords are the Don'ts and our hammers the
   Do's.
Come, children! Get busy! We have no time to lose!

A Letter to Mom

Dear Mom, *I love you very much*,
But I'm too shy to say it,
But now that Mother's Day is here,
I'd better not delay it.

Sometimes I s'pose you'd never guess,
When I am cross and cranky,
Or when I tease or tattle
Or am quarrelsome and pranky . . .

But sometimes when I notice
You are patching clothes at night
Or washing them when I'm in bed
So they will look alright,

Or when you're baking goodies,
Like crunchy cookies brown,
I feel a lump of love inside
I cannot swallow down.

I'm going to try to be the child
You wish I would become,
And then most certainly you'll know how glad
I am that you're *my mom*!

"Dear Mom . . ."

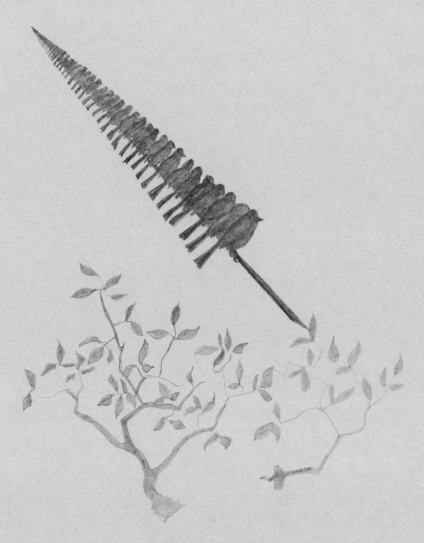

Playing Church

Worship

On a long, long length of a telephone wire,
There perched the singingest kind of a choir.
Two hundred blackbirds—though I did not count
    'em—
Were bubbling with music like springs from a
    fountain,
Singing together. I listened delighted
As more and more birds on the wire alighted.
One must have said Amen! For up from their perch,
Like one bird, they took off. They were done playing
    church.

The Gift

I wonder if the little boy
Who gave his buns away
Knew he'd given them to God
That far-off summer day?
I wonder what he felt like
When he saw each fish and bun
Fed a thousand folks and more,
Enough for everyone.
I wonder, did he think of it
That when he humbly gave
His little lunch to Jesus
Some lives were even saved?
I wonder if the little deeds
I do, or things I give,
Will, by the power of Jesus,
Help others, too, to live?
The things I give seem, oh, so small!
They're just a tiny bit,
But once they're in the hands of God,
He makes *the most of it*.

The Ugly Quarrel

An ugly quarrel showed its face
   and ripped apart some brothers.
It gobbled up their happiness
   and quickly spread to others.
Then someone said, "I'm sorry,"
   and another, "I was wrong,"
And another, "Let's start over,"
   and began to sing a song.

The ugly quarrel wilted.
   Indeed, it lost its punch.
No longer did it rip at joy
   and gobble it for lunch.
A little love and courtesy,
   like sunlight on the frost,
Had melted all ill feelings,
   and the quarrel just got lost.

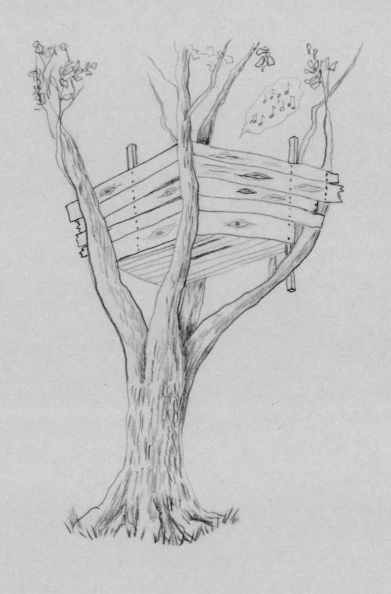

Little Boy in His Tree House

I sit in my wee house
Up in the tree
And quietly listen
To sounds around me:

The clap of the leaves,
The caw of a jay,
The rattle of woodpeckers
Pecking away;

The chirring of beetles,
The hum of a fly
(I'm so far from earth
And so near to the sky!);

The chirp of a cricket,
The buzzing of bees—
I wish that all people
Had houses in trees!

Autumn Leaves

Sparky and I, we tumbled and rolled
in the pile of leaves that Daddy had made.
The dry leaves rustled
    and crackled
        and creakled
            and crunched.
Then down we laid
To see how quiet the leaves could be
if we kept *right still,*
but a small breeze bustled
    and started a riot
of noise in the leaves.
Leaves *can't* be quiet!

Sparky and I have Fun in the Leaves

Candles

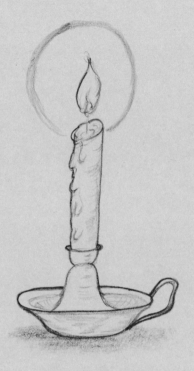

Has your friend a candle?
People see it shine?
Do you sit and glare and sigh,
"Oh! if it were mine!"?

Never blow his candle out.
Leave his light alone.
You can never blow at his
And not blow out your own.

Watch the Things You Say

Watch the things you say, son.
Always you will find
If your words are gentle,
The echo will be kind.

Watch the words you say, son.
Keep them clean and sweet.
They're the ones, without a doubt,
That you will have to "eat."

Watch the words you say, son.
Always keep them true.
Words are like a boomerang—
Words come back to you.

Down-in-the-Mouth

Do you feel down-in-the-mouth?
Does the day seem dark as the night?
You've made a mess of it all
And got yourself in a plight?
Cheer up and think about Jonah—
He made it out alright!

Little Things

One little wire in one little phone
Felt out of sorts and moody and blue.
"I am just one wire, one wee, weak strand,
And there is so little I'm asked to do."

So it gave a jerk. The phone went dead.
A moment later the Fire Chief came
And wanted to quickly call the rounds—
A great, big building had burst in flame!

But the phone was dead! He hollered and tugged
But to no avail. The town was on fire!
Children died and grandmothers cried
Because of one faithless telephone wire.

Dream Clean

Fill your mind with clean things—
Nesting birds, chirping bugs,
Kittens pulling green strings,
Flocks of downy clouds that look like lambs in the
     sky,
Baby's tricks, purple rocks,
Sea-gull's cry,
Shells half buried in the sand,
Tiny chickens in your hand,
Lightning flashing,
Raindrops splashing,
Spiders weaving lacy webs,
Ducklings dunking down their heads.
Fill your mind with clean things,
Things that give your mind wings—
Wash your fancy free of smut.
Lock it tight, keep it shut
to dirty words and gray lies,
Cut your wishes down to size.
Sure, dream!
But dream clean.

Brothers

The Father has children all over creation,
No matter what color they are,
If dark or if light or if shades in between;
They're His children if near or afar.

If they are His children and I am His, too,
Though they're sickly or healthy or shy,
Or if good or if mischievous, they are my brothers—
They have the same Father as I!

Eleven

I've lived so *very* long,
And, oh! so long it seems
Until the magic day will come
When I'll be in my *teens*!

Says Grandma, old and wrinkled,
With wobbly steps and slow,
"When I was young and growing up
Is just a bit ago."

I think Time crawls like snails,
But Mother, with a sigh,
Says like a jet in motion
Time is whizzing by.

I prop my chin and wonder
Why we don't agree,
But, then, perhaps there are some things
That I can't see.

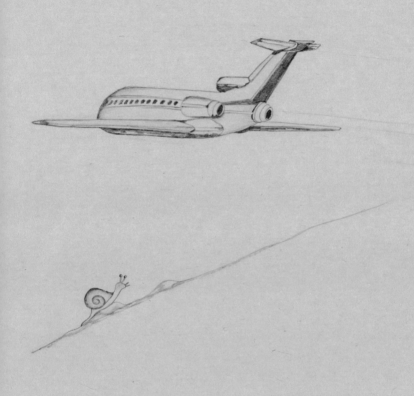

Christmas Question

The little Lord was in a manger born.
His head was cradled in a bed of hay.
The bleating sheep and stolid oxen watched
As 'neath their steaming breath the Baby lay.
If *we* had planned it, where would He've been born?
Not in a barn! A barn is just too odd!
But then where *should* a little lamb be born?
For Jesus was a Lamb—the Lamb of God.

The Shepherd

When David was a shepherd boy,
  he cared for all his sheep.
All day he watched them carefully
  till it was time to sleep.
One day a bear came prowling up
  and gave the lambs a start,
But David grabbed that growly bear
  and broke his jaws apart.

Another time a lion stalked
  behind a little lamb;
Its eyes glowed with a wicked gleam
  that matched his wicked plan.
The lion pounced, but David took
  one mighty, fearless leap.
He tore apart that lion
  and threw him on a heap.

One day this David, now a king,
  sat down and wrote a prayer.
He thought about the lambs, the hills,
  the lion, and the bear.
He wrote, "The Lord's my Shepherd.
  I shall not want." He knew
That, just as once he'd cared for lambs,
  the Lord cared for him, too.

Advice

A rocking chair is good enough
For rocking to and fro,
But it will get you nowhere
If you've got somewhere to go.

So, if the Lord is sending you,
Don't just be a talker,
Don't just be a dreamer,
And, please, get off your rocker.

Two Fellows

I. M. Right was a real disagreeable chap
Who was shrivelled and stunted and small.
He'd swagger and strut and be nasty and mean,
And folks did not like him at all.
I. M. Right kept insisting to others
That he knew far more than the rest,
And no matter what point was in question,
I. M. Right, of course, always knew best.

Could B. Wrong, again, thought he was little;
So he never made very much noise.
He was thoughtful of others and quiet,
Making friends with all manner of boys.

I. M. Right was unhappy and lonely
And somehow just didn't "belong,"
And deep down inside he was wishing
He had muscles like tall Could B. Wrong.
When you take a look at these fellows,
Which one of the two would you like?
The strong Could B. Wrong or, rather,
The little I. (Always) M. Right?

I Like Wheat

I like wheat.
I like the smell;
it's clean and sweet.
I close my eyes and smile
as I dig and slide and swim
in the pile.
I like to catch it in my frock
and pour it out.
I like the way
it sings and rustles
as it gushes from the spout.
I like wheat
slithering 'round my feet.
In fact, I think that wheat
is neat.

I Like the way the Wheat Slithers

Charlie

Charlie has died.
Charlie was my dachshund,
a tiny one, with four short, stubby legs
and big, ploppy feet,
a busy, pointy tail to grin with,
two long ears to flap like flags,
and a smooth, long nose to snuggle with at night.
(I'm only telling you to let you know
how much I loved him.)
He's dead.
After the car had squealed away,
he lay in a mangled little heap.
He didn't even whimper when I screamed.
Daddy dug a hole beneath the cedar.
He laid him in—
gentle-like.
I shut my eyes and ears real tight
so I'd not hear the thud of dirt
on little Charlie.
I wish so much that there'd be puppy-angels
up in heaven.

Charlie Had a Long Wheelbase

Good
Morning,
World

My Window to the Son

It is morning, and I hear the robins chir-ruping
    outside.
I jump from my bed, and I throw the window
    wide.
I am glad the night is over and a new day has
    begun,
And I love to see the morning-world, my window to
    the sun.

I sing and I sing as I start my happy day,
And I take just a little time upon my knees to pray.
For, you see, just like my window, I must open wide
    my heart
To keep it fresh and clean for a good day's start.

In fact, right from the morning until the day is done,
I need to have my window open to the Son.

Night Fears

It is dark, and I am shaking as I creep along the hall.
I stop stalk-still and listen as I flatten to the wall.
Here a shadow! There a shadow! Shadows all
    around!
I wonder, should I make a dash? Or crawl without a
    sound?
"Squeak, squeak!" What is that? What's that
    "thump" I hear?
Oh, my heart is racing! What's that roaring in my
    ear?
Down the hall—slow, soft—up the stairs—creak,
    creak—
What's that moving by the doorway? Ohhh! another
    squeak!
Then with one leap of terror, I dive toward the
    cover;
Safe at last, I'm warm and snug in the arms of
    Mother.
She whispers softly in my ear, "Why, darling! It's
    okay!
God is taking care of us. Don't worry! Let us pray."
She holds me tight and talks to God in whispers by
    my ear.
She asks Him simply to come close and take away
    my fear.

And something happens! I get up, and out the door
   I walk,
And down the stairs and up the hall without a single
   stop!
I wonder where the shadows went? The thumps and
   squeaks are gone!
I saunter to my bed and touch my pillow with a
   yawn.
I snuggle in the covers, all warm with deep amaze
At all the things that happen when a person prays.

To Greet the Spring

There's a tang of Spring on the April breeze.
There's a swelling and a stirring in the maple trees.
There's a choir in the slough in the meadow after
   dark.
The oriole is trying to out-trill the lark.
I feel it and I smell it and I think it's very clear
Wintertime is over and the Spring is here.

Bye for the Summer

Off come our woolies and our mittens fat,
Out come the ball and glove and baseball bat,
Our winter boots are traded for our running shoes,
Off come our coats and the toques we hate to use.
With a splash in a puddle and a robin song to cheer,
Wintertime is over and the Spring is here.

There are twelve chicks chirping, and it's just as I
 had feared—
The cat had seven kittens the day she disappeared!
There's a new calf bawling and a frisky lamb
 romping,
There are five new puppies and a brown foal
 chomping.
The grass is turning green again. The weeds start to
 appear.
There's simply no mistaking it! The Spring is here!

Hi, Spring!

Fathers

I call MY father "Dad."
My dad is kind.
He helps me with the things that are too
        hard for me.
He asks me just to do my best,
And even when I don't (though he is sad),
He loves me anyway.
He cares.
Sometimes when I've been hurt,
I've seen him wipe a tear,
And when I'm happy, Daddy laughs with me.
He understands.
I tell him all that bothers,
And though he doesn't make the world
All right-side-up right now,
He tells me it'll be okay in just a little bit—
And then it is!
He cares enough to spank me when I'm naughty.
He sometimes says a loud, emphatic *no!*
And, other times, a cheerful, smiling, *yes!*
And then, again, when he thinks that it's best,
He tells me, "Wait awhile!"
It isn't what I want, perhaps,
But, then, my daddy seems to *know!*
My daddy does the hard things at our house.
When Mama can't, and I am just too small,
Why! Daddy does it!
He is strong,
And he works hard to give us clothes and food.
I wonder . . .
Jesus talked to God and called Him "Father."
(I think my father's just a little bit like His!)

To Make a Summer . . .

Poems for the 'Tween-ager

To Make a Summer

To make a summer there must be
a blade of grass
a tuft of thistledown
a patch of blue, blue sky
a noisy bee
a lark astonishingly gay
a saucy gopher, busy with his hide-and-seek
a bit of rain
a bit of shimmer on a hot horizon
and, if you want to pare it down
right to the bare essentials,
    one hour 'neath a gnarled old apple tree.

I Know God Heard

The dewdrops glistened in the grass.
I felt the tiny breezes pass.
I felt the bulges, soft and sweet,
Of dandelions neath my feet.
I heard the tinkle of the bells
Of cows in distant, shady dells.
The aspens sylvan secrets told
In whispers on a little knoll.
Two robins in a rhapsody
Of pure delight performed for me,
And from its ferny hiding place,
A freshet leaped in merry race.

So grand the dawn, so sweet the morn,
So glad was I that I was born,
So full that I could not contain
The joy that thrilled me like a pain—
To think that God had given me
Another opportunity!
Another day to laugh, to live,
To think, to feel, to sense, to give!

I knelt. I did not say a word—
Nor needed I. I know God heard.

God is Wise

God is wise. He made the daffodils.
He made the grass that decks a thousand hills.
He made a million things that I can't see;
But, Oh! He thought of everything when He made
    me!
Who else would think of fingernails that grow
And nails protecting each pink, stubby toe?
Who else would think of windows for my head
And make them blue or brown instead of red!
Who else would think of arms to reach for things?
Who else could build a nose to smell the spring,
To catch the scent of flowers in the breeze
And spicy smell of sighing cedar trees!
Who else would plan a mouth so I could eat,
And then a tongue to taste if it is sweet!
Who else, but He, would think of all the fun
That I would miss without two legs to run?
Who else would make the robins on the lawn,
Then give me ears so I could hear their song?

And now I hear Him whisp'ring in my heart,
"Give Me your life, now at the very start."
Oh! Wouldn't I be wrong to tell Him no
When it is He who makes my body grow?
God is so wise! I know, because I see
So much of His great wisdom just in me!

God Made the Daffodils

Lies

The lie you tell in a whisper
When just one friend is about
Is as wrong as the one you tell
To a crowd in an angry shout.

And many who "stretch the truth"
And give a bad rumor wings
Have found that it's like elastic—
When it flies back, it stings.

The wonderful thing about truth,
It's cozy to take to bed!
Best of all, you don't have to remember
Just what it was that you said.

Up-Side-Down Thoughts

I sit and ponder on some things
   that once my Saviour said:
The greatest isn't one who leads
   but one who is gladly led.
The greatest thinks about himself
   as being truly small.
The poor in spirit really are
   the richest ones of all.
The weak are strong. The first are last.
   Who dies to self shall live.
Who keeps is poor, but rich are those
   who give and give and give.
His mathematics aren't like
   the numbers that we use—
But, Oh! how rich His promise if
   His reckoning I choose!
The way He tallies might seem queer
   and even make us frown,
But it is never He, but we
   who are thinking "up-side-down."

Hello, November!

Autumn is going, I know, I know.
There's a hint in the air of coming snow.
The trees stand naked against the sky.
The geese are honking, "Good-bye, good-bye!"
The robins have vanished. The sparrows shiver.
There's a shimmer of mist on the lazy river;
Not a hum a of bee in the browning clover
Is a positive sign that autumn is over.
Good-bye, October! Hello, November,
You gray-brown bridge to a white December!
Not quite warm, and not quite ice—
I think November is rather nice!

On their Way South

Trash Cans

I sat in a corner and counted
    my blessings.
(You see, I had badly
    complained.

I had grumped over dishes
    and bucked about
    mopping,
And, to top it all off, it
    rained;
So Mom made me sit on a
    chair and count blessings.)
Before very long I found
    some,
Besides clothes and food and a roof to live under
And not being blind, deaf, or dumb.
I suddenly thought of the wastepaper basket
Full of garbage and paper and trash
Which soon would be tossed on the burning dump
And be turned into cinders and ash.
I was glad for a place we could put all our junk.
Then I started to think of my wrongs.
I wondered, "Does God have a wastebasket handy
Where the trash in my heart belongs?"
I was sorry I'd grumped. I closed my eyes tightly.
I pretended I saw one, and in
I tossed my complaints, and I asked Him to burn
    them.
And, you know, I got rid of my sin!

On Finding an
Indian Arrow

I stoop to pick a piece of flint
   from the soft dirt upturned,
It's edges keen as any knife,
   an arrow, sharply turned.

Did little Indian lads once play
   upon this rolling field?
And did they shoot these arrows
   from places well concealed?

Did Indian mamas call their girls
   and hungry boys for lunch?
Inside a wigwam made of furs?
   I wonder what they munched.

I wonder if they shook with fear
   when Dad would go to fight
And shoot the dads of other boys
   whose skins (like mine) were white?

I wonder if those children cried
   when Daddy didn't come,
When this small arrow was no match
   for some big, noisy gun?

I found this arrow in the dirt.
   The questions grow and grow.
There is so much about this hill
   that I don't know.

The Gift

"Ribbons and tissue and beautiful bows!
What a beautiful gift! What do you suppose
Is in it?" cried Mary. "I'll open and look!
A picture? Some flowers? A poster? A book?"
Ripping the wrappings, she lifted the box.
Light as a feather! "Is it mittens, or socks?"
She opened. She peeked. She suddenly cried.
There wasn't one thing, no, not one thing inside!

Now can you imagine how Jesus must feel
When, closing our eyes, we will carefully kneel
And use lovely words as we solemnly pray
And yet do not *think* about one word we say?
And think how He feels when we praise Him out
  loud,
Yet inside our hearts we feel haughty and proud;
When we say we are Christians, and yet are unkind;
When we sing with our voices, but not with our
  mind.

Wrappings are nice on a gift, it is true.
But Christ doesn't want wrappings alone—
    HE WANTS YOU.

I Stopped to Watch
a Tumbleweed

I stopped to watch a tumbleweed
  cavorting on a little hill.
A breeze was playing games with it.
  It walked and skipped and hopped, until
It suddenly gave one high leap,
  then started prancing with a wiggle.
It seemed to quiver with delight,
  and I could almost hear it giggle!
Capricious as a naughty sprite,
  hinting of impertinence,
The tumbleweed came to a stop,
  quite suddenly, upon a fence!
"Come play some more!" the West Wind called
  and shook it free! A blue jay cawed.
I gave a little leap of joy—
  I'd shared a happy laugh with God!

One Day in March

A fence post, stark and weathered,
  stood knee-deep in the snow.
The sun was telling winter,
"It is time for you to go."
The fence post leaned forlornly,
  The snow was sagging down,
And if the post had had a face
  it would have worn a frown.
For there it stood, stuck in a drift,
  lean, graying, weak, and stark,
When suddenly, behold!
  A miracle—a meadowlark!
It lighted on that rough, old post,
  fleet and lithe of wing,
And there atop its pulpit,
  I could hear it sing.
It lifted up its yellow throat,
  and it came pouring out—
A flood of liquid melody
  like water from a spout!
Because of it that splintered post
  stood straighter than it had
(I know I just imagined it),
  but things just seemed more glad.
I learned a lesson from the lark
  that early day of spring,
That even if my post is poor,
  it's just the place to sing.

Bones

There are many kinds of bones
Inside the average church,
And, sad to say, for some of them,
You haven't far to search.

One kind I know are JAWBONES
That move with utmost speed;
They're very greatly exercised
In word, but not in deed.
They prattle and they jabber,
But their talk has little to it.
They know so well what should be done,
But they're not those who do it.

Another kind are WISHBONES,
And all of them are fretters.
They sigh about the state of things
And wish the world were better.

Another kind are FUNNYBONES.
When bumped a little wrongly,
They're hurt, and, very touchy,
They feel it very strongly.

And some—we hope they're very few—
Can't hear a thing they're told.
The Spirit left them long ago.
They're DRYBONES, dead and cold.

The TAILBONES are the tardy ones.
They tag along behind.
While other folks are on the job,
They're making up their mind.
They haven't paid their church dues
(Though they intended to),
And while the rest are singing,
They're looking for a pew.

But lots, praise God! are BACKBONES
That hold the vital cord
That binds the Body to its Head,
To Jesus Christ the Lord.
These keep the body straight and strong,
Supple, sturdy, true,
And gladly bend to do God's work.
What kind of bone are you?

A Parable

The imps of hell had a meeting
(Now, you know, this is just a story),
And they bragged of the things they had done,
Vicious and vile and gory.
One had toppled a steeple
Off of an old stone chapel.
One had provoked a lady
By placing a worm in her apple.
But Satan was not delighted,
"Can't you give better reports?"
"I put a long face on a Christian
and made him feel out of sorts,"
Said a third. "That's better!" the devil
Replied with a grin of glee.
"All disagreeable Christians
Are doing their best for me."
"And I," said a dark little demon,
Looking wicked and wierd and wild,
"I went and parked on the shoulder
Of an almost-grown-up child."
"And then?" asked the eager devil
Clutching his evil sword.

"Well, a chap was inviting this youngster
To give his heart to the Lord,
And I sat by his ear and whispered
'You'll not make it anyhow!'
And I finally got him persuaded
To answer 'Later . . . not now.' "
"Yours is the prize!" laughed Satan.
"Keep him as long as you can!
The longer it takes, the better the chance
We'll have him when he is a man."

The Wrong Fountain

You'd think it was awful,
Indeed, quite unlawful,
To drink from a sewer, I know!
You'd shudder with horror
Should anyone pour you
A drink from that odious flow!

Completely unthinkable!
Sludge isn't drinkable!
You'd really become very ill.
Indeed, it would kill you
If someone should fill you
With even a cup of that swill.

It is strange—you will find
Folks will poison their mind
When they never would poison their body.
Strange that, no matter what,
They will feed upon smut
And on books that are filthy and shoddy.

Lots of magazine racks
And most paperbacks
Are just like a sewer, I think.
They're just like a tap
That runs with a sap
From which, no, not one person should drink.

The Bible says, Whatsoever things are pure,
whatsoever things are lovely,
whatsoever things are of good
report, if there be any virtue,
if there be any praise,
think on these things.

Faith

"Except ye become as little children . . . "

"We knew, though no one believed a word
When we told them so," said the little throng,
"From the time He held us upon His lap
That He simply couldn't be gone for long."

"I knew all along," said the little girl.
"I knew when I caught that first, new breath
When He called my name and woke me up,
That He could never be held by Death."

"I always knew," said the little boy,
"From the moment He took the lunch I'd brought
And He fed five thousand with my two fish,
He would always live, no matter what."

But, children, how come *you* understood?
"As simple as *that*! He *said* He would."

Polishing Halos

I had a funny little dream:
Angels round my bed
Hovered happily with each
A halo on his head.
They laughed a tinkling laughter,
A holy kind of glee,
That crowd of lilting angels
Who kept me company!
And all of them were busy
Polishing away—
Each on another's halo,
Till brighter than the day
They glowed with sparkling splendor!
Suddenly I knew
That was the reason for their joy
(A truth from out the blue!).
So now when I'm unhappy,
I look at folks around
And try to see if they, like me,
Are feeling rather "down."
And then I get my polish out
(A cheery word, a song,
A tender touch, a compliment),
and then, before too long,
All of us are happy.
Their halos glow, and mine
(I never guessed till I was told)—
It also gets a shine!

The Difference

Put a fence post in the ground
Where the soil is damp.
Put a little sapling by it,
Hold it straight, and tamp.

A hundred years from now the world,
As it passes by,
Will behold a tall green tree
Reaching to the sky.

But the fence post none will find,
Once so stout and strong.
Rotten, turned to dust and dirt,
It will long have gone.

The sapling was a piece of wood,
But, then, so was the post.
One was dead and one alive,
And that's what mattered most.

Are you grafted into Christ,
   the Living Tree?
The difference will show
   eternally.

No Glass Between

Tim pressed his face against the glass
  and yearned to touch the toys,
But all the fancy things in stores
  were made for other boys.
That teddy bear would be so nice
  to cuddle with at night,
And, Oh! he'd like that bat and ball,
  that Tonka truck, that kite!
But, with his hands in pockets thrust,
  he pushed away his dream.
How come that all the things he liked
  somehow had "glass between"?

Tim shivered in his tattered coat
  and, on his cold, numb feet,
He ran past well-filled windows
  along the roaring street.
His mother would be waiting
  (she was lying sick in bed,
And Dad had not been home for days
  and never brought them bread).
No, toys were just not meant for him,
  nor clothes, nor boots for feet.
Glass always seemed to cover
  everything he'd like to eat.
He wiped his wishing-tears and thought
  of all the "glass between,"
When suddenly a screech of brakes
  was heard, a moan, a scream,

115

And Tim lay on the crosswalk.
  They picked him up for dead.
Kind strangers took his bleeding form
  and laid him on a bed.
The doctors worked. The nurses ran.
  For days Tim quiet lay,
Hovering in Death's shadow,
  his face all bruised and gray.

Then Christmas came, and carollers
  went singing down the hall.
The hospital was showered
  with lots of gifts for all,
And by Tim's broken form they laid
  a teddy bear, a bat,
A Tonka truck, a kite, a ball,
  and other things like that.

That day Tim once again "came to."
  He thought 'twas all a dream;
For if it were not, then how come
  there was no glass between?
He touched the cuddly bear and cried
  to nurses coming fast,
"Oh, how I wish they wouldn't come
  and put him behind glass!
This is the nicest teddy bear
  that I have ever seen.
If I'll pray hard, do you suppose
  no glass will come between?"

The Christmas gift God sent one day
  is open to each one.
There's not a child that does not have
  a way to reach His Son.
The greatest gift of Heaven
  to all the tattered earth,
To torn and broken nations
  around the whole world's girth,
Can be received by everyone.
  His love is not a dream.
To all who truly long for Him
  there is no "glass between."

I Wonder

I saw the picture in the paper yesterday.
A little girl
With huge, black eyes
And arms like knobby sticks,
With great, big elbows
And ribs that looked
Like outsized corduroy.
She leaned against her mother
Just as thin.
Now, when I am hungry,
I tell my mom
I'd like to eat,
And she says, O. K., what shall it be?
Better not ask for anything sweet.
Will a cracker do with a glass of milk?
I wonder,
Did that little girl ask her mommy, too?
And did the mother say,
Will a glass of milk with a cracker do?
I wonder
What does a mother do
Who hasn't one thing to give her baby?
What does she do when her little girl cries
      and cries and cries
        and cries and cries
          and finally
dies?

Kite Thoughts

Someone told me,
Go fly a kite,
and I did.
I pinned a prayer to its sail,
and I ran against the wind,
and it went up to God.
It came back with an answer.
I no longer hated.

Six Sparrows in the Snow

I saw six sparrows in the snow
  and watched them peck and shiver.
A wind was whistling from the north
  that made the outdoors quiver.

It ruffled up their feathers, but
  they didn't seem to worry.
"Never mind!" they chirped with cheer
  amid the icy flurry.

Pausing twixt their rapid pecks,
  they'd tilt their tiny heads,
As though to thank the Lord for food
  and downy feather beds!

They didn't seem to mind the storm,
  nor let the cold winds hinder.
Sparrows must be very brave—
  they stay at home for winter!

They sang in spite of blizzard
  and biting winds that blow.
Today I learned a lesson from
  six sparrows in the snow.

Bible Story Poems

The Awful Bear Story

There's a story of some children
(and it isn't long at all,
just two verses in the Bible—
you might miss them, they're so small)
who were playing by the roadside
when a prophet came along.
They stopped what they were doing
and began to chant a song,
"Baldy, Baldy, you're a Baldy!
Baldy, Baldy, where's your hat?"
Imagine! To a gentleman!
A man of God at that!
"Baldy, Baldy, you're a Baldy.
Baldy, Baldy, go away!"
Oh, how impolite, how vulgar
those children were that day!
BUT
while they yelled their insults,
jeering, shouting, making fun,
two huge she-bears came a-charging
from the forest on the run.
Snarling, growling, grunting, howling,
flailing with their knife-like claws,
they came at those frightened children,
snapping, ripping with their jaws.
Forty-two of them lay mangled

when those vicious bears were done.
No more insults! No more jeering!
No more chanting, making fun.
Does the story give you shivers,
fill your little heart with fright?
It is written in the Bible,
teaching us to be polite.

A Proud Leper Takes a Bath

(2 Kings 5)

Naaman sat on the edge of his bed,
And he looked at the spots on his feet.
He looked at the spots on his elbows and knees
With the awfullest look of defeat.
His wife lay and cried, for bigger and bigger
The spots were beginning to grow,
And before very long—Oh! worst thought of all—
They would certainly start to *show!*
Not a doctor could cure them. No wizards in Syria
Ever could witch them away.
No money could heal them. The spots of the leper
Just grew bigger and bigger each day.
Naaman put on his tunic and medals,
His helmet and sheath for his dagger;
Then, wiping away every trace of a tear,
He walked from his room with a swagger.
Sara, a little slave, went to her lady

Who wept on her ivory bed.
"What's the matter?" she asked. "It is Naaman's
    illness!
The spots just get bigger," she said.
"They will show! He might die! O dear, what to do!"
The little slave pondered a bit.
"A prophet of God in Israel, my homeland,
Could deliver my master of it."
The lady leaped up from her downy soft pillows
And rang all the bells in the palace.
The servants came running from hither and yon,
Each dropping their broom, mop, or chalice.
"Go quickly!" she ordered. "Tell master to come!"
They sought him with frenzy and shout.
Striding indoors, he went to his wife—

126

What was she so frantic about?
She told him what sweet little Sara had said;
He was just as excited as she!
He ordered his chariot! Off to the castle
Ben-hadad, his king, for to see.

The king wrote a letter to Israel's monarch:
"My officer, Naaman, is sick.
We have a report that a man in your land
Can heal him. Now do so right quick!"
Then taking the letter, some servants and silver,
And thousands of dollars of gold,
And ten suits of clothing, proud Naaman went
For the healing of which he'd been told.
The king, being greatest, no doubt was the one
Who'd have power to heal him, and so,

In stately array, to the palace he galloped,
His plume waving grandly for show.
The king of the Israelites met his grand guest.
Slitting open the letter he'd brought
From the king at Damascus, he started to shiver!
Heal Naaman? This he could not!
Leaving the captain, he went in a huddle
And called all his wisest of men.
If they could not heal him, Ben-hadad would come
And invade Israel's cities again!
Tearing his robes and removing his crown
And rolling in ashes and dust,
The king cried in terror, "This man must be healed!
He must! But how? Oh, he must!"
He paced down his corridors, wringing his hands,

Then a messenger came with the word
That Elisha the prophet would heal this proud leper
In the name of Jehovah the Lord.
With a sigh of relief, the king sent his visitor
Off to Elisha. "What's this?"
Exclaimed stately Naaman, "Such a poor house!
I am sure something must be amiss!"
Puzzled, he stepped from his fancy, big chariot,
Knocked on the rough wooden door.
Where were the welcoming banners? the officers?
This had not happened before!
These insolent Israelites! They must be taught
A lesson or two! Yes—but wait!
He had come for a favor! He'd come for a healing!
Still, why must he stand *here* and wait!
The door of the lowly house opened a crack.
A servant peeked out from inside;
Elisha himself was not even coming
To greet him and bid him abide!
"Go wash in the Jordan. Dip down seven times,
And your illness will vanish." Each word
That fell from the lips of the servant seemed foolish.
How beggarly! Stupid! Absurd!
Sir Naaman stomped to his gold-laden chariot.
"Back to Damascus!" he shouted.
"Our rivers are cleaner! Why jump in the Jordan?
You'd think they'd respect me," he pouted.
"I thought that this prophet they prated about
Would come and call loudly and pray
In the name of his God with his hand waving
    grandly,
While my spots all would vanish away!"

129

Back to their country they turned, but his servants
Felt sorry for their leprous master.
Now he'd never be healed! Why did he not yield
'Stead of whipping his steeds to go faster?
At last one spoke softly, "O master, please halt!
Had the prophet performed something grand,
Had he told you to burn seven bullocks for
   cleansing,
Or a whole herd of oxen or rams—
But, now, all he ordered was, 'Wash in the Jordan,'
Why not at least give it a try?
If you're cleansed, praise his God, and if not,
   well . . . er . . . well,
I suppose you'll just suffer and die . . . "
Sir Naaman halted. He pondered and, finally,
Veered his strong steeds to the right,
And down to the Jordan he slowly rode forward.
His retinue watched him alight.
Removing his plumes and his tunic and dagger,
He slowly went down the decline.
He stepped in the Jordan; the water swirled
   muddily,
"What a disgrace! In this slime!"
But down went the head of the Syrian officer;
Out of the water he came.
Why! the spots on his feet and his elbows and knees
Were there, as he'd thought! Just the same!
"Again!" coaxed his servants. Again he went under.
Gray water dripped down from his beard.
The third time! The spots were no smaller, no better,
Exactly as big as he'd feared.
The fourth, fifth, and sixth. "This surely is folly!"

He muttered beneath his wet breath.
" 'Twould surely be better to race to Damascus
A leper—and doomed to death!"
He went for his chariot. "No!" cried his servants,
"Go down just once more. Oh! why not!"
"All right!" growled their master, and down once
  again,
And up—AND THERE WAS NOT A SPOT!
As clean as baby! No trace of an ulcer!

"Back! Back to the prophet once more!"
He shouted, and, whipping his horse to a gallop,
He rode to the same rough, wood door.
"Now I know that your Lord is the God of all Gods!
Take this silver, these suits, and this gold."
"Nay, nay!" said Elisha, " 'twas not I who healed
  you,
And God's gifts are not bought, neither sold."
"Your God will I worship," said Naaman, humbled,
As back to his chariot he trod,
And, as long as he lived, he could never forget
The power of Israel's God.

Two Mites Become Much

(Luke 21:1-4)

Simon, a merchant from downtown Jerusalem,
paused at the foot of the stair.
He glanced at the beggars. "How stupid! How lazy!"
he muttered, and gave them a glare.
"Why must the steps to the temple be littered
with scum like these paupers, I say!"
Then scornfully sweeping right past them, he
    mounted
the steps. He was going to pray.
A nuisance—this business of going to worship
when he could be making a shekel
while selling his wares for a fat, ample profit!
How Simon delighted to heckle!
With his black, beady eyes, he would look at the
    folks
who came to his stall in the market,
and, sizing them up, he would guess what they'd
    pay—
and the top price was always his target!
Now, climbing the stairs, Simon entered the temple
to worship. 'Twas good for his trade.
Why! every good Jew only dealt with good Jews
who tithed all their earnings and prayed!
Looking left, looking right, he paused for a moment
and knelt with his head on the floor.
Then brushing the dust from his good linen tunic,
he strode to the box by the door.
He dug in his pocket and got out some money.

Ah! People were pausing to see!
Then today he would put quite a bit in the poor-box!
Aha! Twenty-two, twenty-three, twenty-four,
    twenty-five,
twenty-six coins of silver!
A lot for a man of his rating!
He dropped them in slowly and carefully
    counted . . .
and the bystanders counted and waited!
"Twenty-six! Dear! How generous!" everyone
    thought
(that is, all who watched, but one Person,
One who knew that in giving to God from the heart,
there was nothing that Simon was worse in!).

Next came old Jacob, a portly old gentleman,
huffing along twixt the pillars
with a flabby, white thumb stuck inside his broad
    sash.
He was chief of Jerusalem's millers.
He bought slaves left and right to do all his
    grinding.
He raked in his money like hay.
When the poor with their pennies would come to
    buy flour,
scratching out their last farthings to pay,
he'd stand by his counter and watch like a hawk—
Every mite that they owed he'd exact.
When they were not looking, he'd quickly dig into
the sack and take some flour back.
Now Jacob's broad tassles that hung from his robe
swept the floor as he chuffed up the aisle.

He greeted the rich as he waddled on past them
and greeted the priest with a smile.
He clattered a coin in the cup of a cripple
who happened to lie in his path.
Holding his nose, he said 'neath his breath,
"Why doesn't the wretch take a bath!"
Then Jacob knelt down on the cool temple floor
and prayed, looking up to the ceiling.
With hands tightly clasped, he recited his prayer
with careful expression of feeling.
That duty accomplished, he went to the box.
Deep down in his pockets he dug
and put in the coins he had counted at home,
feeling good and contented and smug.
Jacob went back to his mills and his slaves
and his moneybags hidden away
and his hungry-faced customers, quite at his ease
that he'd taken some time out to pray.

Next Gershom, a cunning collector of taxes,
came into the temple for prayer.
He was shrewd; he was sharp. He was richer by far
than anyone else who was there.
No matter to him that small children were crying
because he had taken a portion
of gold from their daddies that he had no right to—
a sin that is still called *extortion*.
He twisted the rings on his cold, crooked fingers
as, stiff and correct, he passed by
the poor sweating beggars who lay on the steps,
glancing down with his hard, cruel eye.
What was it to him that their ulcers were oozing

and their elbows were knobby and sore?
So making his way to the temple to pray,
he paused at the box by the door.
Gershom poked round in the pouch that he carried.
"Clang, clang, clink, clink, clang" went the pieces
as Gershom kept shoving the coins in the slot.
"How watchful that ugly old priest is!"
he angrily thought. This was costing a lot!
Oh, well! The peasants had more.
He would just make the tax a bit higher this week,
and he'd soon have as much as before.

A widow edged up to the box by the doorway.
Her face and her hands were all wrinkled,
but her lips held a smile for the paupers she passed
while her gentle eyes happily twinkled.
She stopped for a moment and whispered a prayer,
"O thank You, kind God in the skies!
You give me so much! I have strength! I've a mind.
I can hear. I have two healthy eyes.
I can work, even if it's just scrubbing for others,
and, though I get tired and worn,
I've nothing to grumble about and complain,
nor have had since the day I was born.
Now my debts are all paid, and I've just a bit left,
and so many there are who are poor!
Here is all that I have. It is only two mites,
and Oh! how I wish it were more!"
So saying, she quietly slipped in the coins
and, humming a tune, went her way.
She hadn't a clue there was Someone Who knew
and heard all her heart had to say.

135

Jesus was standing and tenderly watching
as the dear, dark-eyed widow went out.
Then He gathered His friends who had also been
   looking,
and He told them, "There isn't a doubt
about who is the happiest giver who came—
not the rich, who thought that they *had* to,
but the poorly-clad widow who prayed 'cause she
   meant it
and *gave* because she was glad to!"
With a clang and a twang and a showing-off bang,
the rich, of their gold, gave a part.
They went away poor; she went away rich,
Because she gave all she had *from the heart*.

Where Are the Nine?

The road was hot and dusty,
    and the earth was dry and sere.
Ten men lounged by the village wall
    where no one would come near.
Each time that anyone approached,
    they'd raise a weary cry.
"Unclean! Unclean! Unclean!" they called
    to those who passed them by.

Simon, blind for seven years;
    Saul, without a nose!
Stephan had no fingers,
    and Joseph had no toes.
Amos was so crippled
    that he could hardly walk;
Aaron's mouth was damaged so
    he couldn't even talk;
Laban, full of ugly sores;
    Levi, dull, depressed;
And Eli, a Samaritan,
    despised by all the rest,
Made up the crew of ten who roamed,
    unhappy, shunned, and ill.
No hope on their horizons,
    their courage sadly nil.

Forbidden in the villages,
    outcast from hearth and home,
Doomed by the scourge of leprosy
    as aliens to roam.

They scrounged in alleys for their food
    or begged from passersby,
But always when and where they went,
    they raised that rending cry,
"Unclean! Unclean!" O misery!
    Each heartbeat and each breath
a throb of fear and anguish,
    bound by a living death.

And then one day they overheard
    a Man from Galilee
Could heal the lame and deaf and dumb
    and make the blind to see.
They perked right up and strained to hear—
    That Man could even heal
A leper! Oh, how leaped their hearts!
    Could this—could this be real?

And then they heard, O wonder!
    this Man was passing through
The very village where they were—
    if only it were true!

But, lo! next day they heard a stir,
    and, coming down the street,
They saw the One they'd waited for,
    the Man they'd longed to meet.
Those ten, they raised one mighty cry
    and made an awful fuss.
Instead of crying out, "Unclean!"
    they cried, "Oh, pity us!"
The Lord looked with compassion
    upon that motley crew.
The misery of those lepers
    His loving heart well knew.
He said, "Go show the priests you're healed."
    What! Had they heard Him right?
They paused, then of a sudden turned—
    an awe-inspiring sight!
Simon suddenly could see!
    And Saul, what do you know!
The moment he obeyed he felt
    his nose begin to grow!
Stephan counted fingers
    as he hurried to his priest.
Aaron talked nonstop about
    the food on which he'd feast
With his new mouth and lips and tongue.
    And Joseph counted toes,
Which were more beautiful to him
    than Saul's new-sprouted nose!
And Laban felt his lovely skin
    so smooth and all unscarred,
And Levi grinned from ear to ear
    and chuckled long and hard.

Eli, the Samaritan,
 saw his sores disappear.
His heart was overflowing, and
 he wiped away a tear.
He hadn't even found the priest
 as yet. His heart so burned!
He could not wait! And to the Lord
 he suddenly returned.
He threw himself upon the ground.
 Words in a torrent poured,
Mixed with tears of gratefulness
 to his kind, tender Lord.
He kissed those tired, dusty feet
 and threw his arms around
The Master; for his thankfulness
 simply knew no bound.

Then the Samaritan ran off
 to show with bated breath
That he, a leper, had been healed—
 snatched from a living death!

The sun was setting in the west.
 The moon began to climb.
"I healed ten lepers," Jesus said.
 "But where, where are the nine?"
Does Simon not know how to praise?
 Does Saul not think to thank?
Is Joseph, too, ungrateful?
 Is Stephan's heart a blank?

Does Amos not remember
    this morn he couldn't walk?
Does Aaron, with his new-made tongue,
    naught of thanksgiving talk?

Now Jesus' searching question
    comes to your heart and mine,
"Ten children I have helped today,
    but where, where are the nine?"

The Story of a Poor Rich Man
and a Brand-New Beggar

Solomon Simon once lived in a palace,
the grandest and richest in town,
with patios, porches, and playgrounds and pools
and beautiful parks of renown.

Lazarus, again, was a poor, starving beggar
with only some rags around him.
He lay at the gate of rich Solomon's house,
where a lone little puppy-dog found him.
It licked at the sores upon Lazarus' elbows,
his shoulders, his knees, and his feet.
Then, having no master, the dog lay beside him
on the hard, chilly stones on the street.
Lazarus snuggled up closer for warmth.
He wished he had something to offer
the poor little pup. It was hungry, like him,
and he hated to see it suffer.

Lazarus hadn't had breakfast,
    nor dinner,
      nor supper,
        nor even some bread.
For days now he'd begged at the gate of that palace,
too sick to go elsewhere instead.

Solomon Simon would grandly ride past
on his chariot fancy and high.
He'd glance at the beggar a moment and mutter,
"Poor wretch! 'Twould be good if he'd die."

Lazarus sometimes would open his eyes,
watching Solomon while he dined,
and then he would crawl 'neath the big, laden table
to see if a crumb he could find,
But always a guard or a butler would come
and kick him aside in the grass.
"Beat it!" they'd shout to the cowering beggar.
"Make way for the scullers to pass."

One night poor Lazarus no longer cared.
Sick, starving, and chilled to the bone,
he whispered a prayer to the God of his fathers
and died on the cold cobblestone.
The angels of God came to take him away
(though they left his cold *body* behind).
They took him to Heaven to Abraham's bosom
—Father Abraham, gentle and kind.
God gave to Laz'rus a body, brand-new!
And a mansion in Heaven forever,
Where he'd never have tummy-aches ever again
and no suffering whatsoever.

Lazarus' body—the *old* one, the *cold* one—
was picked up and carted away.
No flowers! No tears! Not even a coffin!
And no people to follow and pray.
Just one little puppy-dog followed the cart
On which the body of Lazarus lay.

Solomon Simon that night had a party,
a supper so big 'twas a fright—
venison, veal, roast mutton to *start* with!
His brothers and he dined all night.
The brothers—five of them—also were wealthy
and sinful and selfish, each one.
They cared not for God, and they cared not for men,
but just for their money and fun.

Solomon Simon leaned back after supper,
so fat and so full that he burped,
groaning with all of the food he had gobbled

144

and all of the wine he had slurped.
Solomon Simon then called for a jester
who made them all roar with laughter.
Then twenty-two dancers and seventeen singers
were called to come in right after.
But suddenly Solomon Simon got sick—
so sick that he bellowed with pain!
His wife called the doctor who came on the double,
but, Oh! he hurried in vain!

Solomon Simon's poor soul left his body
(in other words, Solomon died).
His wife fell and fainted. His brothers lamented.
They tore at their beards, and they cried.

They had a grand funeral with hundreds of wreaths
and a coffin of marble and gold.
Then Solomon's *body* was put deep down
in a sepulchre musty and cold.

And the *soul* of poor Solomon Simon went down,
    down,
      down
        to a place called Hell,
there in the darkness and fire and torment
forever and ever to dwell.

Now Hell was not *planned* for people to go to,
but for *evil* and *Satan* and *sin*,
but those who love evil and do not love God,
why! that's where they choose to go in.

Solomon Simon rolled in the darkness
and cried with a terrible thirst.
No wine, and no water! Nothing but sorrow—
and forever! That was the worst.

Looking up, far, far up, the poor rich man saw
    Laz'rus
in Abraham's arms sweetly dreaming.
"Water! Cold water, one drop on my tongue!"
begged Solomon angrily screaming.
"Send that beggar down with one drop of cold
    water."

"He cannot come," Abraham said.
"There's a great, wide, uncrossable gulf in
    between
you and us," and he shook his head.

Solomon Simon thought of his life.
Too late of his sins he repented.
"Send prophets, send preachers, send Bibles, send
    teachers,"
the poor rich man sadly lamented.
"Send Lazarus back from Heaven to warn
all my sin-loving, self-loving brothers,
and tell them to spend all the rest of their lives
in living for God and for others."

A Time for Singing

Accept our Thanks, O Lord

M. P. T. (Thanksgiving) Margaret Penner Toews

O Lord, to Thee our grate - ful hearts we raise,
For warmth of hearth and ten - der - ness of home,
For or - chards with their sweet - ly la - den trees,
For Christ who gave His life to save our own,

U - nit - ing in a psalm of prayer and praise
For love that friends and fam - i - ly have shown,
For cat - tle on the lush and roll - ing leas,
For par - don for the wrong that we have done,

To thank Thee for Thy prov - i - den - tial ways,
For all the hap - py times that we have known,
For har - vests from the rip - pling, gol - den seas,
For Heav - en when the crown of life is won,

AC - CEPT OUR THANKS, O LORD.

While the World Was Sleeping

M. P. T.   (Christmas)   Margaret Penner Toews

While the world was sleep-ing, while the night was still,
To the dis-tant seek-ers, yearn-ing from a-far,
Still to seek-ing wise men in the world's dark night

To the faith-ful shep-herds on a qui-et hill
There ap-peared the glor-y of a bril-liant star,
And to faith-ful watch-ers, Lo! there comes a light

Came the won-drous mes-sage of a mir-a-cle:
Beck-'ning to the sta-ble with the door a-jar:
And a mes-sage ring-ing from the God of might:

Chorus

Je-sus Christ is born! Come and wor-ship Him!

Has-ten now re-joic-ing un-to Beth-le-hem.

152

Sing about Jesus

M. P. T. Not too slowly   (Christmas)   Margaret Penner Toews

Sing, sing, sing a - bout Je - sus on Christ - mas morn;
Sing, sing, sing of a Sav - iour to all who sin;
Come, come, come to the man - ger to see the King;

Tell, tell, tell all the world that a King is born.
Tell, tell, tell all the world He gives peace with - in,
Come, come, come to the man - ger your gifts to bring.

Sing of the star in the mid - night sky; Sing of the an - gels
Peace in a world that is bruised and torn, Peace for each heart that
Bring Him your loy - al - ty; bring Him your heart; Bring Him o - be - di

Slower . . . .

who came from high; Sing of a lit - tle ba - by's cry.
is all for - lorn, Peace, for the Prince of Peace is born.
ence from the start; Then un - to others His love im - part.

Tell all the world of Him.

153

The Golden Rule

(Round Song)

1. There is a rule in the game of life to fol-low if you'd be true:
2. Sim - ple and clear is the gol-den rule giv - en by One who knew:

1&2 { "Do, do, do un - to oth-ers as you would have them do to you."

The Rainstorm

(Round Song)

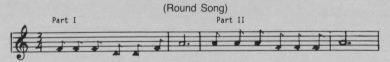

Flicker and glim-mer and flash, Mut-ter and rum-ble and crash,

Pit-ter and pat-ter, sputter and spat-ter, Rat-tle and pour and roar.

154

Lift Your Lamp

(Round Song)

Lift your lamp. Hold high the flame.

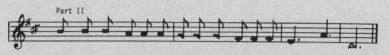

Throw out the bush-el that co-vers your can-dle in Je - sus' name.

My God Is My Refuge

(Round Song)

My God is my re - fuge; He keeps me from harm,

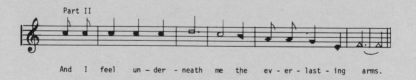

And I feel un — der - neath me the ev - er - last - ing arms.

The Puppy Parable

M. P. T.

Margaret Penner Toews

Once there was a lit - tle pup-py in a par - a-ble I heard
O this hy - per-ac - tive pup-py, he would yelp and yip and yap
Then one day that lit - tle puppy, when his mama told him, "Don't!"
O his snout was full of stickers, and his paws were full of pricks,
Now that pup-py's learned his les-son! He's improved an aw-ful lot.

Who did - n't like to lis-ten and who would - n't heed a word
And go chas-ing where he should-n't with a snarl and snip and snap
And his pa-pa barked, "Now listen," which he an - swered with, "I won't,"
And his lips were barbed and bleeding with those wick - ed lit-tle sticks.
When his ma-ma barks her or-ders, he is "John - ny - on-the-spot,"

That the ma - ma pup - py ut - tered, and I tell you, it was sad;
Till the ma - ma pup - py cried to Pa - pa Pup-py, "O boo-noo!
That ob - noxious lit - tle pup - py chased a prick - ly por - cu-pine.
How that naughty pup - py wished that he had lis - tened to his dad.
For that por-cu - pine has shown him, in the sharp-est kind of way,

He would - n't e - ven lis - ten to his shag - gy-coat - ed dad.
Al - phon - so, dar-ling, tell me, what will we have to do?"
He screamed, "Ow, ow, ow, ow, ow," and let an aw - ful whine!
He whim-pered to his ma - ma, "I'm sor - ry I was bad."
For a pup-py's health, it's bet-ter to lis - ten and o - bey.

156

I'm Happy Today

M. P. T.

Margaret Penner Toews

There's a rob-in chirp-ing in the map-le tree In the middle
of the rose there sits a bum-ble bee, And I doubt that a
day could ev-er nic-er be, And I'm hap-py to-day!

There's a sun-beam danc-ing on my win-dow sill And a lamb
a-leap-ing on the west-ward hill; It will be a love-ly
morn-ing. O I know it will! I am hap-py to-day!

There's a God in Heav-en watch-ing o-ver me And the Bi-
ble says He loves me ten-der-ly, And I love Him,
too, with ev-ery part of me; So I'm hap-py to-day!

My Pony and I

M. P. T.

Margaret Penner Toews

Swift - ly o'er mea - dow and hill - ock we gal - lop, my po - ny and I.
Rab - bits and go - phers go hur - ry and scur - ry as po - ny and I,

My po - ny and I, sail - ing o - ver the grass - y prair - ie,
My po - ny and I, pass by their bur-rows and trails with a flur - ry

We fly, we fly. Thun - der of hoofs on the turf, we go, Leav - ing
On by, on by. On with a gal - lop, the wind we face. Up the

a trail of dust, we know, gal - lop-ing, gal-lop-ing, o-heigh-o,
hill, down the dale, on we race, gal - lop-ing on at a glorious pace,

My dear lit - tle po - ny and I.

I Want to be a Christian

M. P. T.

Margaret Penner Toews

I want to be a Christian, yes, I do! I want to be a Chris - tian
I want to be a Christian, all the time; I want to walk a - right and
I want to be a Christian to the end, A Chris - tian with a help - ing

thru' and thru'! In a crowd or when a - lone, at the mar - ket
toe the line, Be - ing hon - est, be - ing kind, leav - ing sel - fish -
hand to lend, Lov - ing oth - ers, friend or foe, sooth - ing pain and

and at home, Ev - ery day till it has flown, I would be true.
ness be - hind, With a hum - ble, rea - dy mind, yes, all the time.
eas - ing woe And where - ev - er I may go, His loy - al friend.

Chorus

Nev-er de - vi - ate, Nev - er vac - ci - late;
Nev - er turn a - side, Ev - er in the truth a - bide;

In as much as li - eth in me, I'll be true.

Samson

M. P. T.

Margaret Penner Toews

Called to be judge was tall Samson of old, Powerful,
Samson marched boldly to conquer the foe, Caught thirty
Samson came riding, by Philistines bound. "Snap" went the
Then came a maid with beguiling dark eyes And with a

fearless and famous and bold. Samson had muscles and hair
foxes to tie in a row. Tails all ablazing with fi-
rope; then a jawbone he found. When he was done with the bone
tongue that told smooth little lies. When all the foe failed to catch

you could twine. All that he lacked was a powerful spine.
re they came, Setting the Philistines' barley aflame.
of the ox, One thousand Philistines littered the rocks.
whom they sought, Samson by little Delilah was caught.

(Faster)

Samson! Samson! Better obey God's plan!
Samson! Samson! Better obey God's plan!
Samson! Samson! Better obey the Lord!
Samson! Samson! You didn't obey God's plan!

Samson! Samson! Muscles don't make the man.
Samson! Samson! Wits don't make the man.
Samson! Samson! Don't you trust your sword!
Samson! Samson! Muscles don't make the man.

160

My Friend

M. P. T.

Margaret Penner Toews

Oth - er friends may fail, but Je - sus nev - er will. Oth - er friends
Oth - er friends, when winds un-kind be - gin to blow, Might be - lieve
Oth - er friends can't al - ways un - der-stand my plight Nor the joy

may van - ish; He is with me still; Other friends are hu - man and,
the worst of me and say 'tis so; Other friends might not for-give
that thrills me when my heart is light. Other friends are dear, but, Oh!

like me, are frail; Je - sus is the on - ly One who will not fail.
nor wrongs for - get. Je - sus is the kind-est friend I've ev - er met.
'tis good to know Je - sus won't forsake me, for He's told me so.

The Bible Tells Me So

M. P. T.

Margaret Penner Toews

There are some folks who'd have me think the world be - gan by chance,
The same folks tell me I e - volved from mon-keys long a - go,
So care-ful-ly God planned it all, each a - tom and each cell,

That the stars that in their or - bits swing are a mat - ter of hap-penstance,
That it is just an ac - ci - dent how the fruit and the flowers grow.
Each germ of life, each snow - flake, and each leaf that in au-tumn fell.

That once there was a won - drous "Bang" And then in place they fell,
I don't know how they do it; It takes more 'faith,' by far,
He fash-ioned it from no - thing! He spoke, and it came to be!

And all earth's liv - ing crea - tures grew from a ran - dom cell.
To think it all 'just hap-pened,' than whence things real - ly are.
And to those who don't be - lieve it and tell me diff'- rent - ly,

But
And I just smile, 'cause there's some - thing that I know! The world was made

by a God of love, For the Bi - ble tells me so.

Sound of the Wind

M. P. T.

Margaret Penner Toews

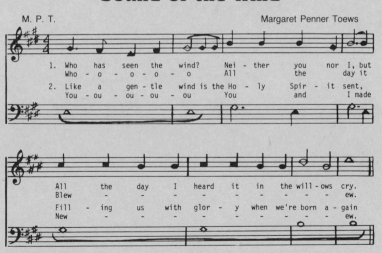

1. Who has seen the wind? Nei - ther you nor I, but
   Who - o - o - o - o All the day it
2. Like a gen - tle wind is the Ho - ly Spir - it sent,
   You - ou - ou - ou - ou You and I made

All the day I heard it in the will - ows cry.
Blew - - - - - - - ew.
Fill - ing us with glor - y when we're born a - gain
New - - - - - - ew.

I Stand at the Gate

M. P. T.

Margaret Penner Toews

I stand at the gate of my life, and a-head There are choices
I'll fol - low the Lord while I'm young and strong, For He's giv - en
Tho' Sat - an might whis - per and tempt my heart A - side in -

that face me, I know; There are roads I can tra - vel to wealth
His life for me. It's a choice that I know I will not
to by - ways of sin, The Fa - ther has prom - ised that in

Chorus

and fame, But they're roads I don't want to go. Lord, guide me in
re - gret, Now nor in e - ter - ni - ty. Lord, guide me in
the pow'r Of His Son I shall sure - ly win.

mak - ing my choice. Lord, help me to heed Thy voice and ev - er

in Thee re - joice, and my life will be one of joy.

Index

Where Is God?

To Make a Summer . . .

Bible Story Poems

A Time for Singing